I Like Giving.

THE 7 WAYS OF LIVING GENEROUSLY

Give, share, and show you care.

GENEROUS THOUGHTS: Use a thought in my mind to think something kind.

GENEROUS WORDS: Use what I say to make someone's day.

GENEROUS MONEY: Use my money — no matter how much — if there is a life I can touch.

GENEROUS TIME: Use any moment in my day to put Generosity on display.

GENEROUS INFLUENCE: Use the choices that I make to affect the actions other people take.

GENEROUS ATTENTION: Use my eyes to see and ears to hear. Listen well and distractions disappear.

GENEROUS BELONGINGS: Use what I have to share — I can do this anywhere.

Ellie the Elephant and the Stinkin' Thinkin'

Copyright © 2023 by I Like Giving.®

Author Betta Tugive is the pen name for the I Like Giving.® Writing Team.

Scripture taken from the International Children's Bible®. Copyright © 1986, 1988, 1999, 2015 by Thomas Nelson. Used by permission. All rights reserved.

All rights reserved. No part of this book may be reproduced or transmitted in any form or by any means, electronic or mechanical, including photocopying and recording, or by information storage or retrieval system, without permission in writing from I Like Giving.®

Printed in the United States of America 2023.

ISBN 979-8-9880723-3-1

**Dedicated to Bill and Sherri —
Big-hearted givers.**

I Like Giving.® Writing Team:
S.F. Aughtmon
and friends

Illustrated by
Ben Cole & Andy Towler

Special thanks to The Marion and Bob Taylor Family

ELLIE THE ELEPHANT
AND THE
STINKIN' THINKIN'

BY

Betta Tugive

I Like Giving. Publishing
Colorado Springs, CO

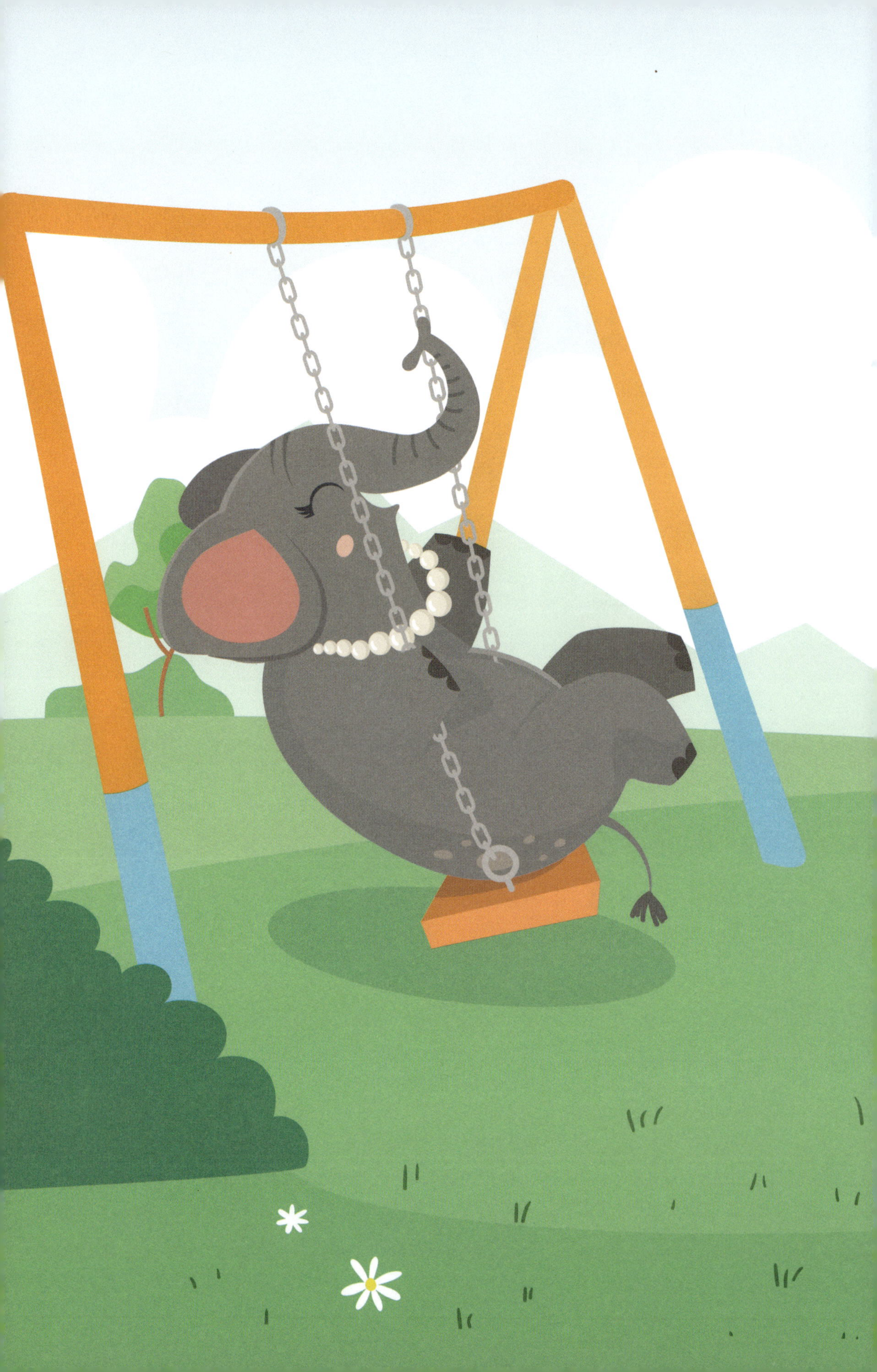

In the land of the givers, where they like to share,
a great thinker was swinging up high in the air.

Ellie's thinker was thinking.

She aimed for the sky.

With her head in the clouds, Ellie felt she could fly.

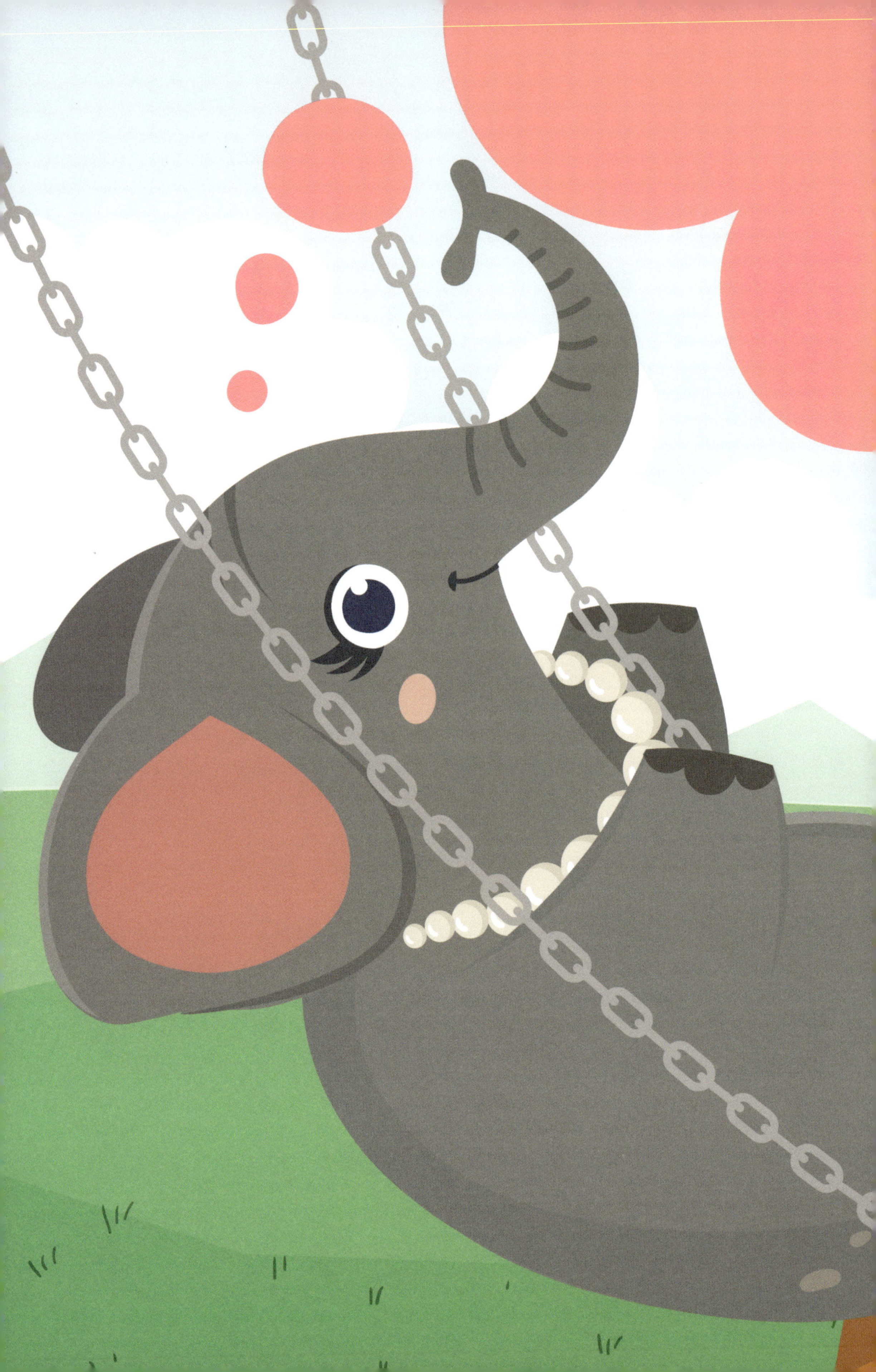

Oh, I love all my friends!
And my friends all love me!
Oh, I love this fun park!
And I love this big tree!

Ellie's thinker was warm.
So, she had a new thought.
I would love an orange popsicle.
It's getting hot!

Yes, a popsicle's perfect
right here in the sun.
I think orange is the best.
It's my favorite one.

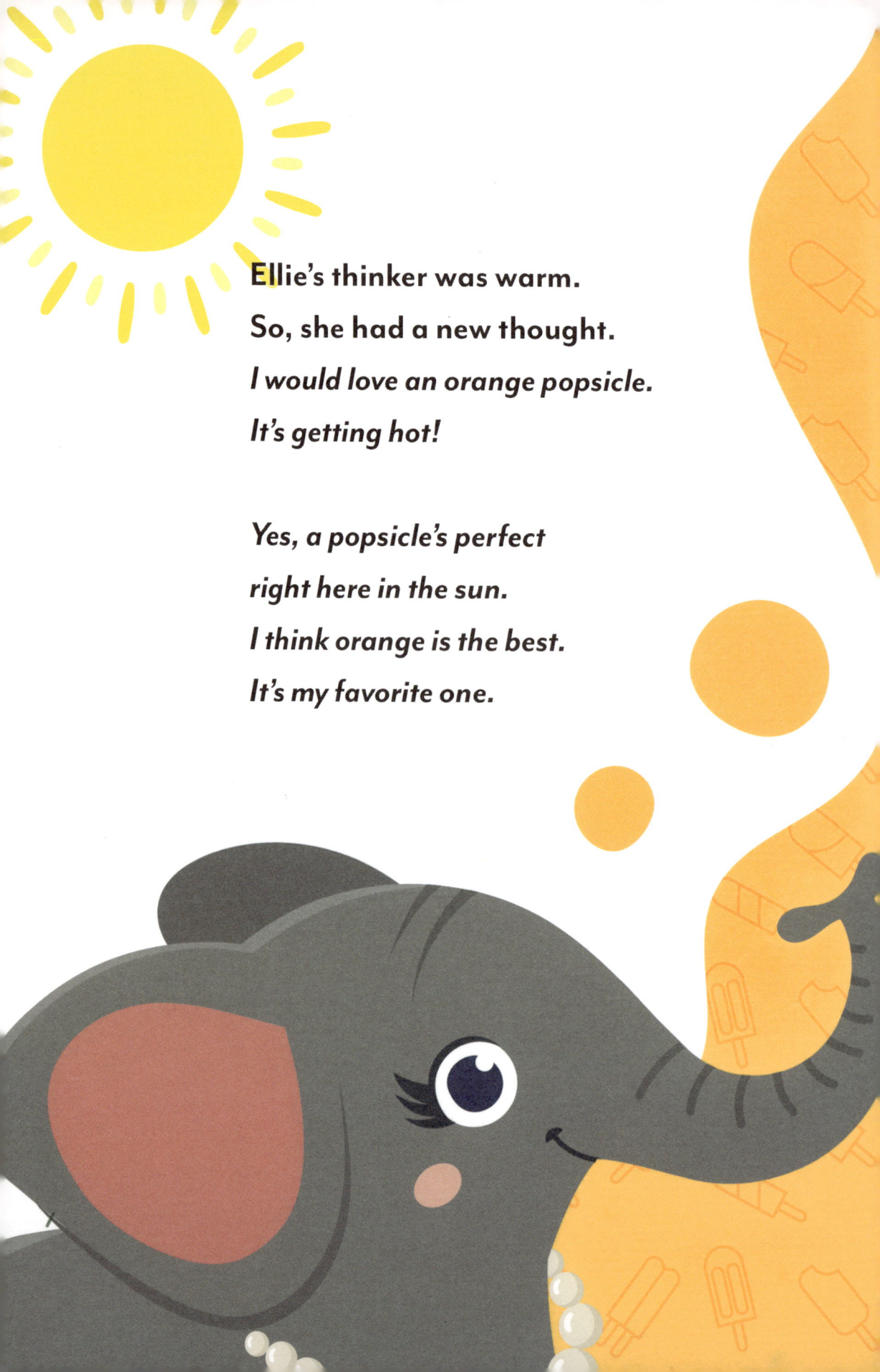

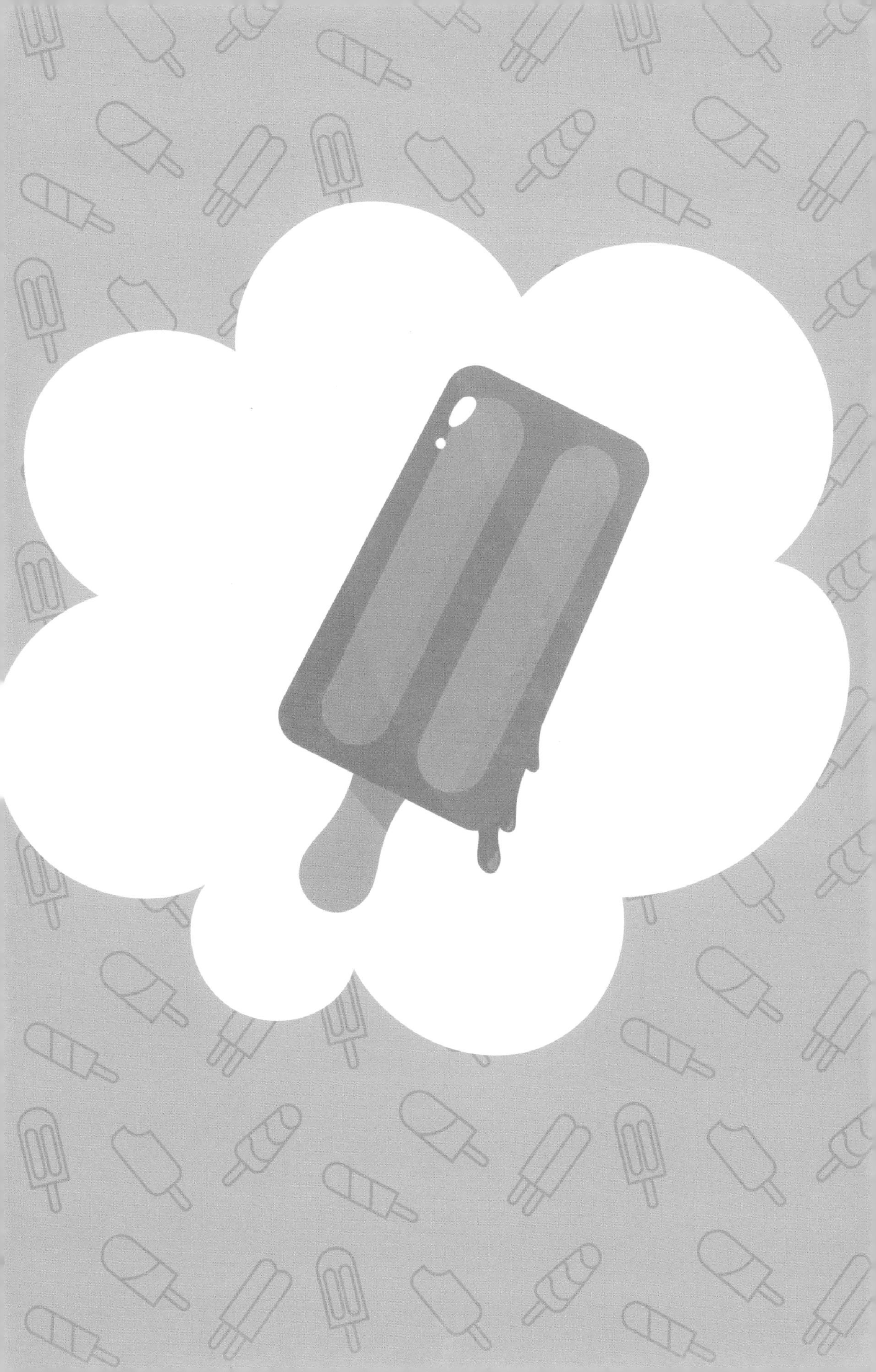

Then her best friend — dear Koko —
she bounced on the scene,
with her pack filled with treats
that were fit for a queen.

With a shout, Koko called,

I've got GREAT treats for all. Have an icy cold snack if you're big or you're small.

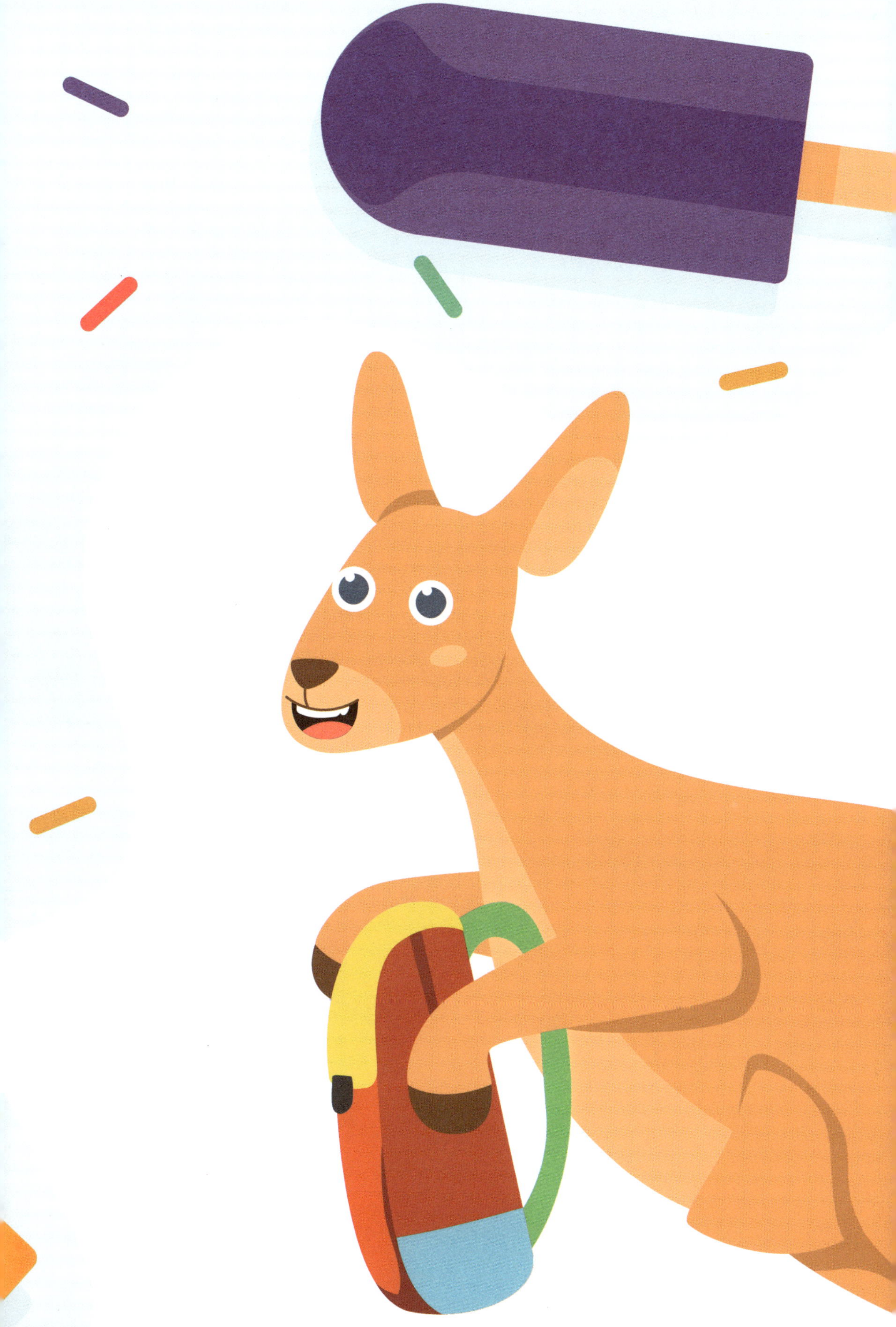

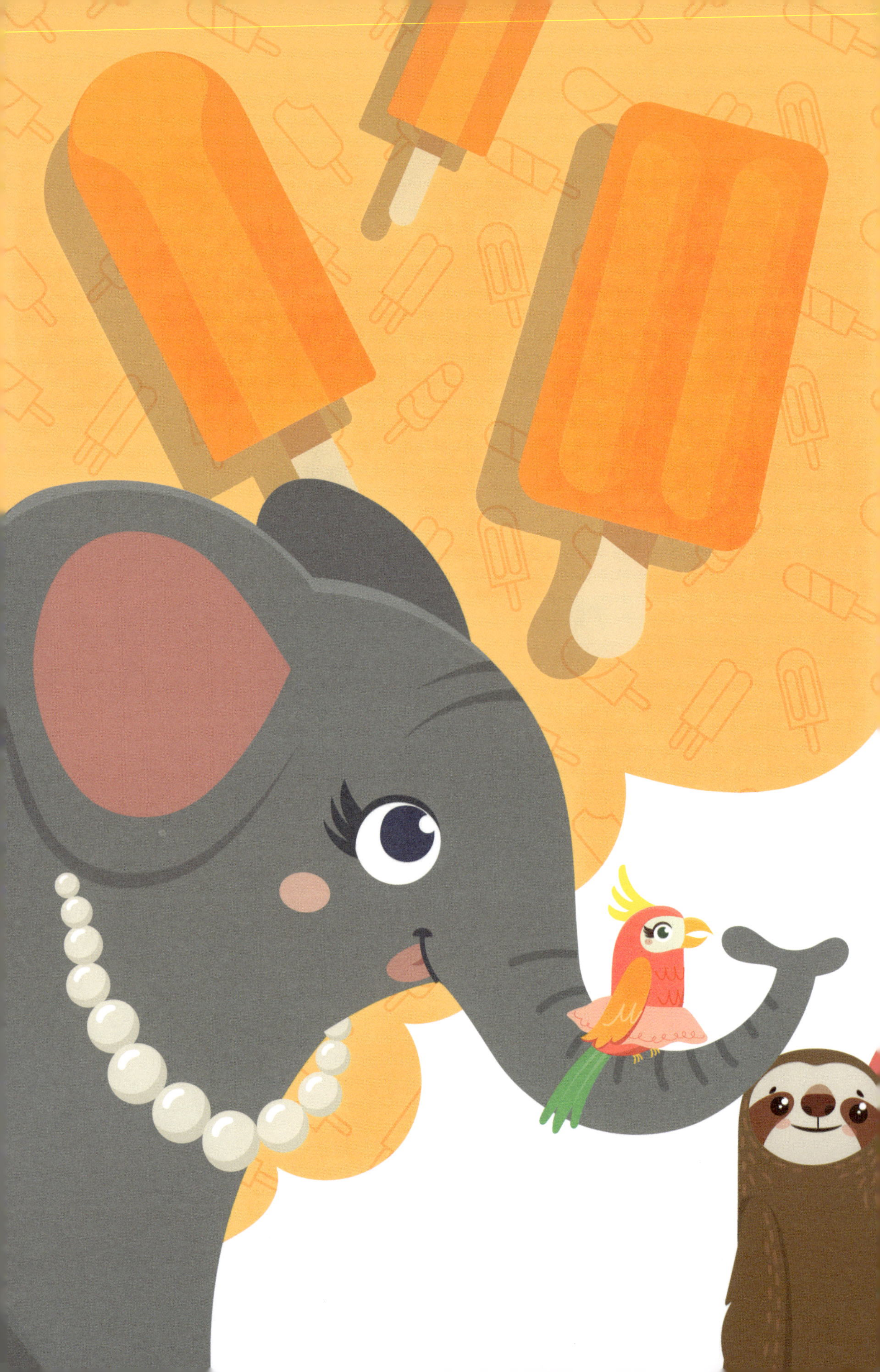

Ellie thought happy thoughts.
Koko really came through!
My orange popsicle dreams
are about to come true.

All her friends got their pops.
Ellie waited in line.
"Can I please have an orange?
It's the very best kind!"

"Oh, I'm sorry, sweet friend."
Her best pal shook her head.
"Yep, I'm all out of orange.
Would you like **GRAPE** instead?"

Ellie's thoughts took a tumble.
They sank really low.

What — no orange?
That's the worst!
What a shame!
What a blow!

Koko knows I love orange.
So she just doesn't care.
Oh, she just doesn't like me.
She's never been fair.

Koko's mad and upset.
Yep, she thinks I'm the worst.
And so that's why she gave
all the orange away first!

Ellie's uncaring thoughts
were so bad that they stunk.
Ugly thoughts filled her head
from her ears to her trunk.

But her good thoughts pushed back. Oh, they put up a fight!

Are you sure that is true?
Hey, now, that can't be right!
All these mean thoughts are lies
and they stink up the joint.
Here's the truth.
KOKO LOVES YOU.
And that is the point.

Those big, generous thoughts,
well, they squeezed their way in —
where the muddled-up, mean,
stinky thoughts once had been.

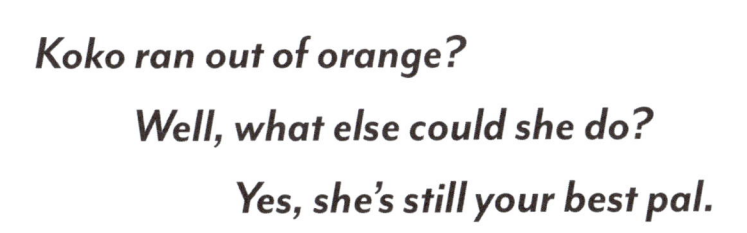

Koko ran out of orange?
Well, what else could she do?
Yes, she's still your best pal.

Stinkin' thinkin'? You're through!

Ellie took the grape treat,

took a lick, and said,

"THANKS!"

Koko, you are so nice! And mean thoughts are for cranks!

See, my thoughts got all stinky,
forgot I was blessed...
**You are caring and kind.
And I think you're the best!**

**You should know that
I LOVE YOU!
And those are the facts!**

Thanks for thinking of others
and sharing your snacks.

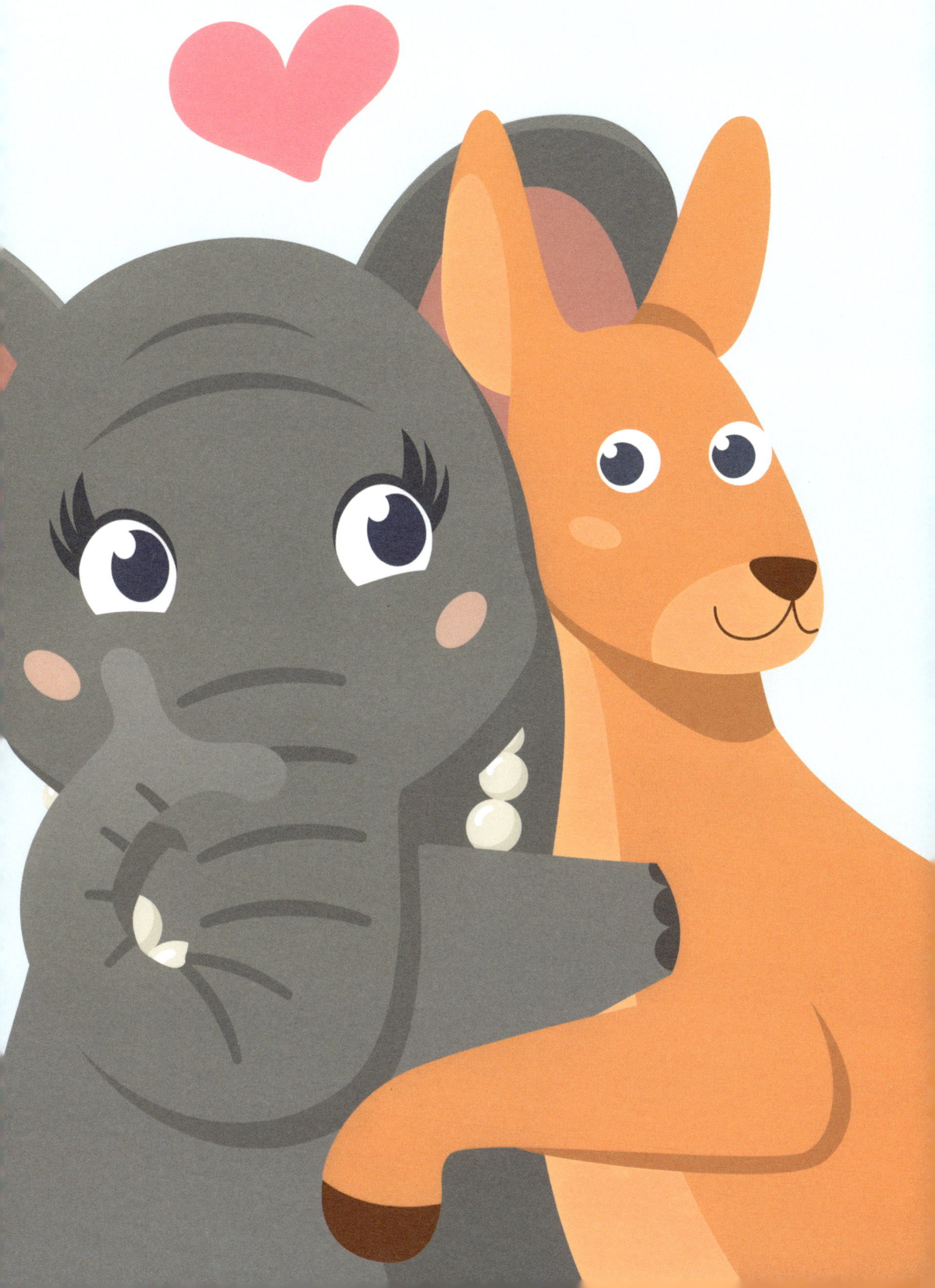

Now, my friend, stop and think.
How is your thinker now?
Is it full of great thoughts
or quite stinky somehow?

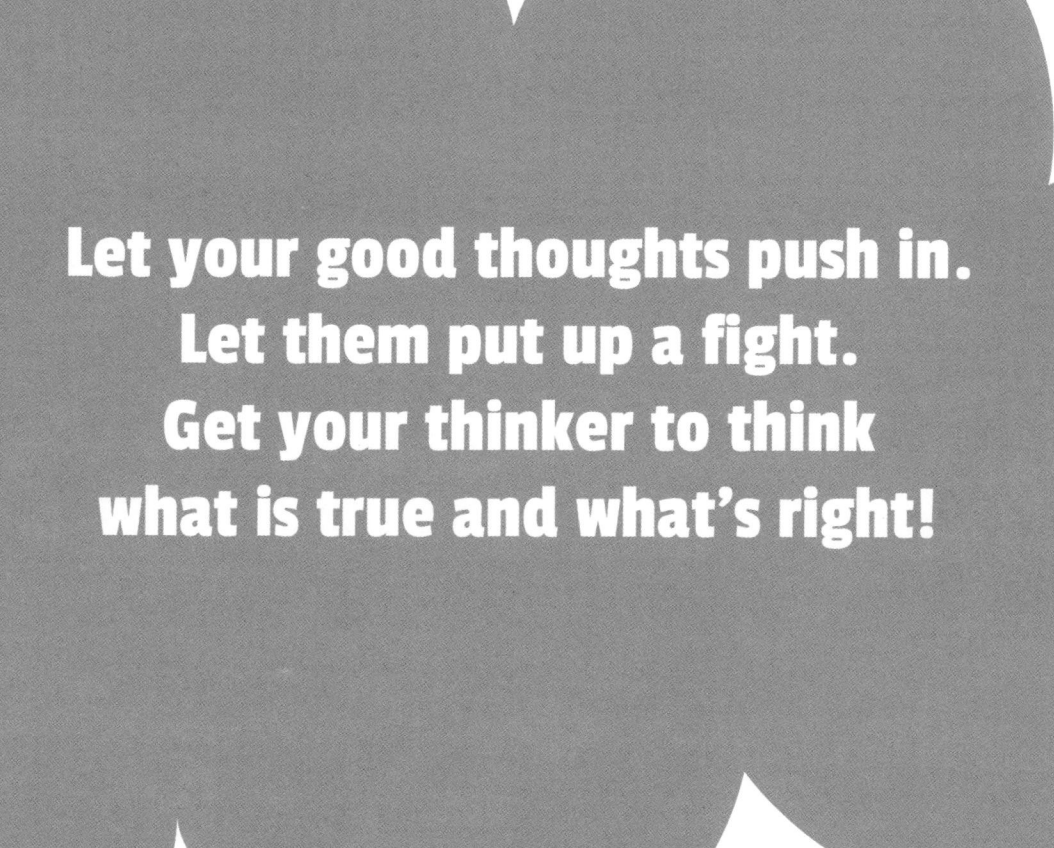

Let your good thoughts push in.
Let them put up a fight.
Get your thinker to think
what is true and what's right!

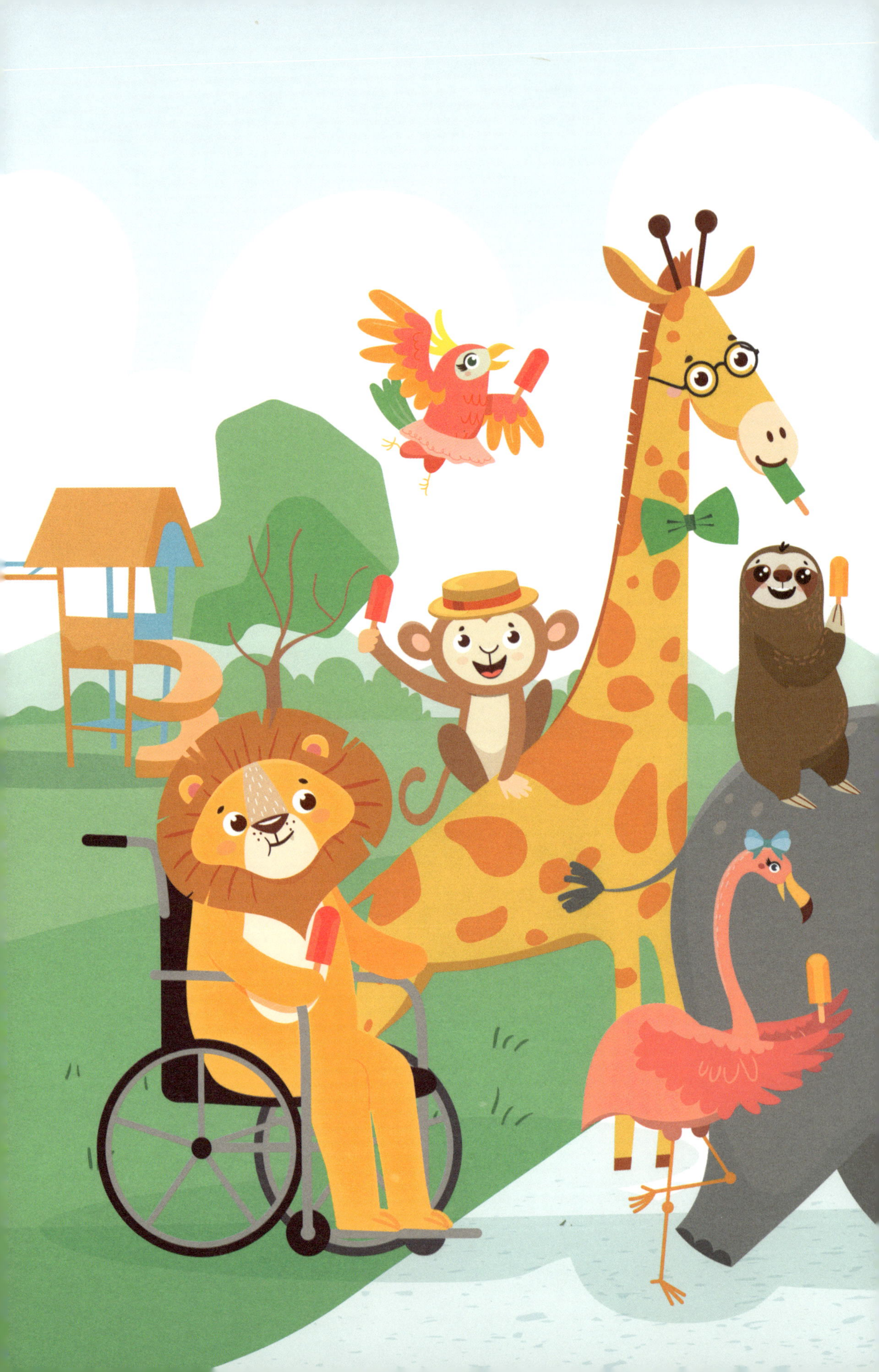

Tell your mean stinkin' thinkin' —
Take off! Go away!
And let's all give a cheer!
Generous Thoughts saved the day!

Talk About It!

How did Ellie's stinky thoughts make her feel and act?

When has Stinkin' Thinkin' caused you to get upset and what did you do?

When can you tell your Stinkin' Thinkin' to take off and go away? What Generous Thoughts can you choose instead?

Giving Challenge

Stinkin' Thinkin' Challenge
This week when you notice stinky thoughts creeping into your mind, say, "Stinkin' Thinkin', take off!" and focus on Generous Thoughts.

Not-My-Way-But-That's-OK! Challenge
Rather than saying —"That's not fair!"— when things don't go the way you want, look for moments when you can say, "Not my way, but that's OK!"

Think about the things that are true and honorable and right
and pure and beautiful and respected.
Philippians 4:8 (ICB)

Visit **generouskidsbookclub.com** to get Ellie's story, meet our other Jungle Friends, and join our monthly book club!

GENEROUS STUDENTS™
HOMESCHOOL EDITION

Join the Generosity Road Trip! **Generous Students™: Homeschool Edition** explores The 7 Ways of Living Generously for all age groups!

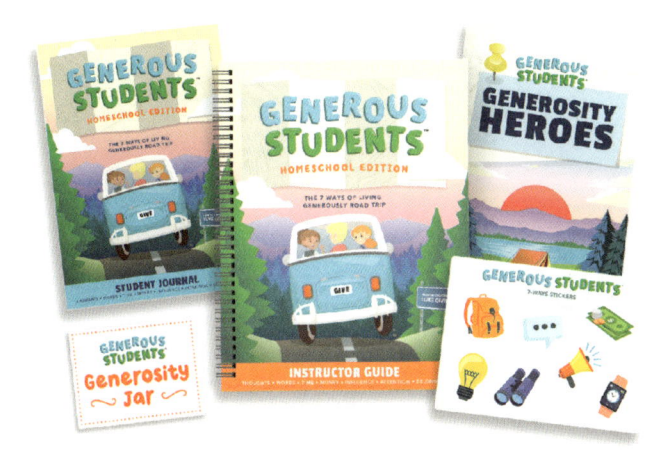

GENEROUS FAMILY™

generousfamily.com

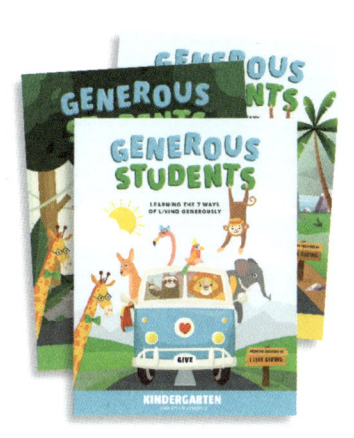

Check out our K-8 faith-based, biblical SEL curriculum! Generous Classroom™ is sharing the importance of gratitude and teaching the next generation how to be life-long givers!

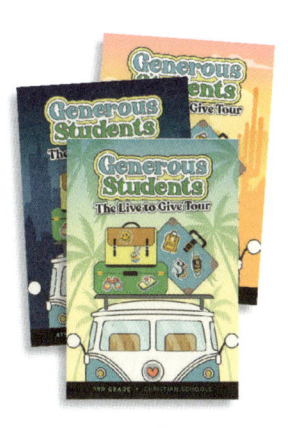

K-2

3-5

6-8

GENEROUS CLASSROOM™

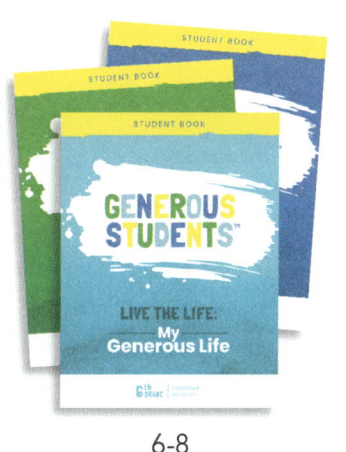

generousclassroom.com